# ELIZABETH

# ELIZABETH

## REIGNING IN STYLE

### JANE EASTOE

PAVILION

First published in the United Kingdom in 2012 by
PAVILION BOOKS
10 Southcombe Street, London W14 0RA
An imprint of Anova Books Company Ltd

Design and layout © Anova Books, 2012, Photography © see acknowledgements, p.112.

Commissioning editor: Emily Preece-Morrison
Cover and concept design: Georgina Hewitt
Copy editor: Nina Sharman
Picture research: Emma O'Neill

ISBN: 9781862059481

A CIP catalogue record for this book is available from the British Library.

10 9 8 7 6 5 4 3 2

Colour reproduction by Rival Colour Ltd, UK
Printed and bound by Toppan Leefung Printing Ltd, China

www.anovabooks.com

COVER: A strapless, "cabbage leaf" dress of finely gathered black taffeta, by Norman Hartnell. The diamond necklace was a wedding present from the Nizam of Hyderabad. Copies of this image were circulated to embassies around the world and appeared on stamps and bank notes. PAGE 2: The Queen wears a tulle evening gown decorated with sprays of wattle – the national flower of Australia – and gold paillette, designed by Norman Hartnell for her two-month Commonwealth tour of Australia in 1953. On her head is the Queen Mary tiara, or "Granny's tiara", about her neck a diamond necklace, a gift from the Nizam of Hyderabad, and pinned to her sash is a bow brooch, a gift from her grandmother, Queen Mary.

# CONTENTS

HARDY AMIES Ltd
14 Savile Row. W.1.
Telephone                              Regent 0788

H.A. 1.

Evening dress in blue/gray heavy satin,
entirely embroidered in a design of autumn leaves
and berries in gold thread and pearls. The wide
skirt is lightly boxpleated at the waist. The
fitted bodice is finished with cuffs of plain
satin, which also makes the stole.

ABOVE: This dress was worn by the Queen at a State dinner given by President and Mrs Eisenhower in 1957. The designer, Hardy Amies, recalled that Her Majesty "shimmered" amongst the guests who included Barbara Hutton, Ginger Rogers and Doris Duke.

# ✦ INTRODUCTION ✦

When Elizabeth Taylor arrived theatrically late at Buckingham Palace for a ceremony in which Richard Burton was being honoured by the Queen, Her Majesty later wryly commented to her milliner Frederick Fox: "What Miss Taylor failed to appreciate is that in this instance everyone had come to see me." As he notes, there was no vanity in this observation, but a simple statement of fact.

Queen Elizabeth II is the most photographed woman in the world. Her path from Princess, to Heir Presumptive and onto Queen has been scrutinized in newspapers, magazines and on television across the decades. The Queen remains the centre of attention wherever she goes and is subject to critical assessment every time she sets foot in public. The pressure of such continuous scrutiny must be phenomenal, yet in sixty years on the throne she has not put a sartorial foot wrong; there has never been a wardrobe malfunction, at least none that the public has been aware of, nor a fashion faux pas. Her impeccable personal style, and skill in resisting fashionable excess, has ensured that her place as a style icon is finally being recognized by leading fashion commentators.

The often repeated assertion that the Queen isn't interested in clothes, was first fostered by Marion Crawford, governess to both Elizabeth and Margaret. In her book *The Little Princesses,* she observes that Princess Elizabeth was not picky about her clothes: "Lilibet never cared a fig. She wore what she was told without argument, apart from a long, drab mackintosh which she loathed." Others maintain that the Queen is at heart one of the old school, a countrywoman who does not care about her appearance.

But this is a myth that should be dispelled: "The Queen is not interested in high fashion", observes one couturier[1], "but she is *very* interested in her clothes and is *very* particular. Her Majesty is acutely aware of how invasive the press are – her clothes are part of her armour. And, after a whole lifetime of wearing couture, she knows exactly what she is doing and makes it perfectly clear when things aren't quite right."

The Queen's clothes reinforce the message that she is a national figurehead with power and status, and must always maintain her authority and emphasize her position. To describe her wardrobe as expansive, and the task of her dressers as considerable, is something of an understatement; consider that on her first Commonwealth tour alone the Queen took 100 specially designed, new outfits. There have been in excess of 170 further Commonwealth tours since then, as well as many other State visits.

Yet, Her Majesty has worn hand-me-downs, had her mother's clothes altered to fit her and worn off-the-peg oufits: on a Commonwealth Tour of Bermuda in 1953, her Coronation year, she wore a Horrockses dress. But principally she has worn couture: that is, clothes designed for her, fitted precisely to her and in her own choice of fabric – one-offs.

At the start of her reign she favoured fairy-tale ball-gowns, or stiff satin frocks, shimmering with beads in patterns designed to emphasize her status. Norman Hartnell, a master with duchesse satin, created two of her most iconic dresses; her wedding dress and her Coronation gown. He specialized in fabulous evening gowns, but his first design for her was in 1935 and he continued until his death in 1979. Hardy Amies started designing for the Queen in the early 1950s and continued until a year before his death in 2003. While he made many beautiful evening gowns he was credited with transforming her day wardrobe with sharp, beautifully tailored coats, dresses and jackets. "I think Hardy always saw her as the beautiful twenty year old he started dressing in 1952", notes a colleague, "and of course she had an amazing figure and a tiny waist for years." Ian Thomas, who had worked for Norman Hartnell, produced softer designs throughout the 1970s and 1980s and Maureen Rose who in turn had worked with Thomas, continued to design for Her Majesty after his death until the late 1980s.

John Anderson received Royal patronage from the late eighties until his death in the late 1990s and his work was continued by his colleague Karl Ludwig Rehse who still designs for Her Majesty. Her youngest couturier is Stuart Parvin, who was first commissioned to design for the Queen in 2000 and he also continues to work for her. Other couturiers are utilized too, all firmly vetted by the palace before any contact is made.

Throughout history the Royal wardrobe has been maintained by a team of dedicated staff. Margaret MacDonald, a formidable Scottish lady fondly known as Bobo, started in service as Princess Elizabeth's nursery maid, graduated to personal dresser when the Princess reached sixteen and remained in the post for a remarkable sixty-seven years; she even accompanied the Princess on her honeymoon. Currently Angela Kelly; Personal Assistant, Advisor and Curator to Her Majesty The Queen, is in charge of a team of dressers. The Queen's dresser is a unique position, she has an intimate relationship with Her Majesty – no one else sees the Royal person in a state of undress, save her husband and her doctor.

The cost of creating and sustaining such an expansive wardrobe is substantial. Her Majesty commissions new clothes for significant events, but wears them over and over again to a range of functions. Great care is taken to ensure she never wears the same outfit to annual events. Hardy Amies received a stack of letters from his Royal patron over the years, some regarding his invoices: "Thank you for the enormous bill which will take a little time to pay", she wrote, clearly feeling the pinch. Cost was, and is, a significant concern. In 1969 Prince Philip declared that the Royal family were "almost in the red", prompting a review of the Civil List, the Labour MP Emmanuel Shinwell observed: "If we want a monarchy we have to pay them properly. We can't have them going around in rags."

But Her Majesty is not complacent about the cost of her clothes: "She was quite thrifty", a *vendeuse* observes, "sometimes a dress would come back to us to be let out so she could wear it again." And a letter to Hardy Amies in late December 1971 also reveals that she had to be scrupulous in her accounting: "I meant to ask you today and stupidly forgot a question of the account. Do you think it would be possible to have the new clothes and the purchase tax on one bill and the other alterations on a second one? I cannot get the Privy Purse to accept my word for the purchase tax, as the item is not put separately on the account." Today couturiers are asked to submit an estimate of the cost of constructing a design, and a discount may be requested by her Household.

It is worth mentioning that Her Majesty is in a uniquely difficult position when it comes to making a critical assessment of her clothes. It is said that until she was thirty Her Majesty lived in a bubble of uncritical adulation and few are brave enough to venture an honest opinion for they are aware that it will not be well-received. However, the couturier Maureen Rose observes in Brian Hoey's book, *Life with the Queen*: "The Queen is very modest with a complete lack of vanity, she only looks in a mirror to check that everything is as it should be, not because she wants to see how good she looks." Her clothes are part of her job and quite unique, for above all else they must always make her look like what she is: The Queen.

# PRINCESS

"THE FUTURE QUEEN HAD LESS FREEDOM OF CHOICE IN WHAT SHE WORE THAN MANY OF HER SUBJECTS. THERE WERE SO MANY RESTRICTIONS, EVEN THOUGH COST WAS NOT ONE OF THEM." ANNE EDWARDS

# PRINCESS

What clothes are deemed fit for a Princess? The Royal family agreed that Princess Elizabeth, born on the 21st April, 1926, should not be brought up in luxury; nevertheless her layette was handmade from the finest materials. But, as if to strike a chord with the nation, it was revealed that the Princess' paternal grandmother, Queen Mary, her mother, the Duchess of York and her maternal grandmother, Lady Strathmore, had personally stitched the said layette themselves.

As a baby and toddler Princess Elizabeth, or Lilibet as she was known, was dressed exclusively in the most impractical colour – white, but as she grew up these frilly dresses were replaced with more practical garments. Despite the four years difference in their ages, when Princess Margaret was taken out of her baby whites, the two Princesses were dressed identically; hand-smocked and pin-tucked dresses, and velvet-collared coats for best, sensible sweaters and kilts for play. They both hated wearing hats and would snap the elastic under each other's chins to cries of "you brute".

According to Lilibet's governess, Marion Crawford, the girls could not have been more simply dressed. "They wore cotton frocks, mostly blue with a flower pattern, and little cardigan coats to match when it was cool." Her nurse Clara Knight, known as Alah, was said to believe that the Princesses were much too simply dressed: "I don't think Alah ever quite approved of the simple lives the little girls led, or their almost severe wardrobes … their plain tweed coats, business-like berets and stout walking shoes", notes Crawfie. Alah could only indulge her fondness for more regal clothing on special occasions producing what Marion Crawford describes as: "two dear little figures like dolls, all organdie frills and ribbons and bows". Lilibet's only jewellery was a coral necklet, a pearl necklace from "Grandpapa England" and a silver bracelet, a gift from her parents; these items were reserved for best.

Although the clothes were simple, it's worth noting that "simplicity" has a different meaning in Royal circles. On her fourth birthday Princess Elizabeth nearly caused a riot when crowds spotted her walking across the square at Windsor Castle in a pretty yellow coat trimmed with fur.

PREVIOUS PAGE: Sixteen-year-old Princess Elizabeth is photographed at Buckingham Palace in October 1942, twelve-year-old Princess Margaret had an identical dress. ABOVE: The three-year-old Princess Elizabeth steps out in a frilly white dress, the inevitable white socks and silver shoes. Her pearl necklace on a platinum chain was a gift from her father who gave her new two pearls on every birthday. Her style is typical of the way that "nice" young girls were dressed in the 1930s, a look that was to continue up to and into the 1950s.

Norman Hartnell made his first dress for Princess Elizabeth in 1935. Both Princesses were to be bridesmaids at the marriage of their uncle, HRH the Duke of Gloucester, to Lady Alice Montagu-Douglas-Scott. The girl's dresses were made of pale pink satin and ruched tulle, and were designed to be ankle-length, but Hartnell was advised that the Princesses' grandfather, King George V, wished that the little ones would be in short dresses: "I want to see their pretty little knees", so the dresses were altered according to his wishes and were later utilized for a trip to the pantomime.

The first serious Royal ceremony that Princess Elizabeth attended was her parent's Coronation on 12 May 1937. Special gold coronets were constructed for the girls, lined in crimson velvet and edged with ermine. However, when the King, Queen and Queen Mary examined them, they were deemed too heavy and ornate. Instead lightweight, silver-gilt coronets, in the style of medieval crowns, were commissioned and declared far more suitable. Margaret bounced so much on the day of the Coronation that at one point her coronet tilted down over one ear.

The Royal library contains an essay by Elizabeth, written in pencil, in which she describes her outfit: "Now I shall give you a description of our dresses. They were white silk with old cream lace and had little gold bows all the way down the middle. They had puffed sleeves with one little bow in the centre. Then there were the robes of purple velvet with gold on the edge."

According to Marion Crawford, the Princesses wore identical dresses to garden parties: "usually of tussore silk, often hand smocked, quite short with knickers to match", a tradition that continued until Elizabeth's thirteenth birthday, when she had grown as tall as her mother. Now silk stockings replaced white socks (the Queen had given her daughter a box of silk stockings as a gift for her twelfth birthday), hemlines were lowered and the girls were no longer made to wear matching outfits. The diarist Chips Cannon thought it odd when he saw the Princesses still dressed the same at a Thanksgiving Service in 1945, Elizabeth was nineteen at the time.

It is clear from the photographs of both Princesses during the war that their clothes were typical of the somewhat drab utility clothing worn by most women. Like everyone else they were "making do", as Cecil Beaton discovered when he photographed Elizabeth just before her nineteenth birthday: "I was bidden to the Palace to see the Princess' dresses, which were hung for display around the walls of her bedroom. Of all those we photographed ... the most successful was the pink spangled crinoline which was one of her mother's pre-war dresses, now altered to fit the daughter."

PREVIOUS PAGE: A six-year-old Princess Elizabeth and her two-year-old sister Princess Margaret develop their love of horses in their maternal grandparents home in August 1932, Margaret is still in whites, but Elizabeth has graduated into print dresses. OPPOSITE: Norman Hartnell's very first design for Princess Elizabeth was a bridesmaid dress when she was just nine years old. Queen Mary declared: "We are very pleased. We think everything is very, very pretty." ABOVE LEFT: King George VI and Queen Elizabeth take eleven-year-old Elizabeth and seven-year-old Margaret for a Coronation concert devised for the Princesses. ABOVE RIGHT: Princesses Elizabeth and Margaret in the garden of the Royal Lodge Windsor, with their mother in June 1936. The girls wear lace-fronted dresses in the Bavarian style that was still acceptable pre-war.

ABOVE: Princess Elizabeth acted as bridesmaid to her uncle, the Duke of Kent and Princess Marina of Greece in November 1934. OPPOSITE: According to Marion Crawford, there was only issue with the Coronation clothes: "We had one scene when Margaret found Lilibet was to wear a little train, while she had none." Both wear cloaks edged in ermine. Both Princesses wear pearl necklaces, gifts from their grandfather King George V: Elizabeth's has three strings to Margaret's two.

OPPOSITE:  The fifteen-year-old Princess Elizabeth is photographed with her sister Princess Margaret and their dog Chung at the Royal Lodge, Windsor, on 11 April 1942. The Princesses wore almost identical outfits two years earlier to make a radio broadcast on "Children's Hour" and we know that Margaret often wore Elizabeth's hand-me-downs. ABOVE:  Princess Elizabeth plays the piano at Windsor in June 1940 in a typical war-time print dress, as usual her younger sister had an exact replica.

ABOVE LEFT: Princess Elizabeth wears a nautical-inspired design on board HMS Implacable on a visit from HMS Vanguard – note her hat – on the Royal tour to South Africa in 1947. ABOVE RIGHT: In 1945 at eighteen years of age, Princess Elizabeth joined the Auxiliary Territorial Service. She dressed the same as everyone else, although as one fellow servicewoman commented to Brian Hoey in his book *Life with the Queen*: "Her uniforms were better tailored than ours, and even her overalls were pressed and laundered every day."

ABOVE: Princess Elizabeth was made Colonel of the Grenadier Guards in 1942, Cecil Beaton marked the occasion with a portrait of the Princess in uniform with her hat worn at a jaunty angle. The hat caused a sensation, it was widely copied and "The Princess Hat", as it was known, became a bestseller.

ABOVE: Dispelling the myth that Royalty never wear the same dress twice, Princess Elizabeth first appeared in the above dress on the Royal tour of South Africa and later wore it in some of her engagment pictures as well as in this formal portrait, suggesting it was a favourite dress. OPPOSITE: Princess Elizabeth is photographed in 1945 by Cecil Beaton in a Norman Hartnell dress. It was originally made for her mother pre-war but, in the spirit of "make do and mend", was altered by Hartnell to fit her.

# WIFE

"THE GOLDEN RULE IN ROYAL DRESSING IS THAT CLOTHES MUST BE
COMFORTABLE, BECOMING AND ACCEPTABLE. THE FIRST CANON OF GOOD TASTE
IS TO DRESS IN A WAY THAT IS FITTING FOR THE OCCASION. A QUEEN DOES NOT
DRESS TO IMPRESS. HAVING NO SOCIAL SUPERIORS SHE DOES NOT NEED TO."
COLIN MCDOWELL

# WIFE

Born in 1926, Princess Elizabeth Alexandra Mary's style has always been definitively English and aristocratic, from the sensible coats worn for public occasions, to the formal dress she wore for her father's Coronation in 1937, she was never fussy, flouncy or overdressed. Nonetheless, the young Princess learned early that hats and crowns were an essential feature of her wardrobe.

According to Marion Crawford in her book *The Little Princesses*, it was not until the year before she became engaged that Princess Elizabeth was allowed for the first time to select her own dresses: "Lilibet's taste in clothes followed her mother's closely. She chose mostly pastel shades, and was from the very first attached to silk or thin wool frocks, with coats that matched exactly. For evening frocks she mostly chooses very full skirts of the picture kind. Wisely, for these suit her admirably." As a teenager Lilibet's clothes were made by Miss Ford of Handley Seymour, who also made Queen Mary's clothes. Norman Hartnell, who was to be commissioned to create Princess Elizabeth's wedding dress, was already a favourite with both her mother and her grandmother. The simple cream dress that Princess Elizabeth wore for her official engagement photographs (see page 24) could easily have belonged to her mother, so similar was the style. But fashion in the post-war days was austere, and it was a look that was to dominate until the launch of Dior's New Look in Paris, 1949.

When it came to the wedding dress, however, Princess Elizabeth was very much in charge. A number of designers were selected to submit sketches for the wedding, planned for the 20 November, 1947. In August, Hartnell heard that one of his designs had been selected from the twelve he had submitted, leaving him with under three months to complete the dress. This was a time of rationing and Princess Elizabeth had famously saved up her ration coupons for the occasion. Hartnell ordered the silk satin he required to make the dress from a Scottish firm, but questions were immediately asked of the prime minister as to the provenance of the worms used to make the silk. There was concern so soon after the war that the nationality of

PREVIOUS PAGE: Originally published in *Picture Post*, this photograph of Princess Elizabeth arriving at Westminster Abbey shows her being fussed over by her bridesmaids like any other bride. ABOVE: One of a series of engagement photographs of Princess Elizabeth and Lt. Philip Mountbatten on 11 July 1947. The Princess was allotted an extra 100 clothing coupons for her wedding, with bridesmaids and pages also being given extra coupons for their clothes.

the silkworms might be from unpatriotic sources, such as Italy or Japan, but Hartnell was able to allay fears with the information that the dress fabric was made from: "Chinese worms – from Nationalist China", while the silk for the train was woven by Kentish silkworms.

Embroidery was a feature of Hartnell designs and obtaining the required pearls for the wedding dress caused the couturier something of a headache. Hartnell's manager, Captain Mitchision, was despatched to the United States and when asked on his return if he had anything to declare, whispered that he had: "ten thousand pearls for the wedding dress of Princess Elizabeth". The pearls were held at customs until the duty was paid. Hartnell, with his head-embroideress, traced out the intricate embroidery pattern by hand in pencil on 15 yards (13.7 metres) of tracing paper. Hartnell observed: "Wherever there was space or a weakness of design I drew more wheat, more leaves, more blossom of orange, syringa or jasmine." Three hundred and fifty women worked on the dress for seven weeks to have it ready in time. It was delivered to the palace in a 4 feet (1.2 metre) square box the night before the wedding.

The dress was described in an official press release: "A Princess Gown of Ivory Duchesse satin, cut on classic lines with fitted bodice, long tight sleeves and full falling skirt. The broad heart-shaped neckline of the bodice is delicately embroidered with seed pearls and crystal in a floral design. From the painted waistline, formed by a girdle of pearl and embroidered star flowers, the swirling skirt is hand embroidered in a design inspired by the paintings of Botticelli, representing garlands of White York Roses carried out in raised pearls entwined with ears of corn minutely embroidered in crystals and oat-shaped pearls. Alternating between the garlands of roses and wheat, and forming a final border around the entire hem of the skirt, are bands of orange blossom and star flowers appliqué with transparent tulle bordered with seed pearls and crystals.

A full court-train, 15 feet (4.5 metre) long, of transparent ivory silk tulle attached to the shoulders, is edged with graduated satin flowers, finally forming the deep border at the end of the fan-shaped train. A reversed type of embroidery, as used on the Wedding Gown, is here employed on the train by the use of appliqué satin star flowers, roses and wheat, further encrusted with pearl and crystal embroideries. A voluminous Bridal Veil of crisp white tulle is held by a tiara of pearls and diamonds."

ABOVE LEFT: In July 1951 Princess Elizabeth took the place of her father on a visit to Canada and the United States and, along with Philip (now the Duke of Edinburgh), indulged in some square dancing at Ottawa Government House – the Royal dressers rushed to buy a circle skirt for Princess Elizabeth and a checked shirt and jeans for Philip – a price tag was in evidence revealing the hasty purchase. ABOVE RIGHT: The Princess in a cotton print dress and straw hat on a warm July day in 1951, note her favoured peep-toe, white platform shoes, with ankle straps.

On her feet the Princess wore open-toed, platform shoes, covered in the same material as the dress. The heels were higher than she usually wore and the silver buckles on the shoes were studded with tiny pearls.

Yvonne, the *vendeuse* at Hartnell, who went to help Princess Elizabeth into her dress, later reported that a last minute panic had ensued when the bride's bouquet of white orchids had gone missing. Neither bride nor king knew where it was, a footman remembered receiving it, but most of the palace staff had been allowed to wait in the forecourt to see the bride leave. It was eventually uncovered in the porter's lodge where it had been left to keep cool. There was a similar upset over a missing pearl necklace that had been sent to St James's Palace by mistake to be displayed among the wedding gifts. Princess Elizabeth's Private Secretary was sent to retrieve it, but the policemen on duty at St James's were not convinced by his tale. Eventually they were persuaded to return to Buckingham Palace with him to ensure that he was not a jewel thief.

The bride and groom departed on their honeymoon to Broadlands in the early evening in a chilly, open-topped landau that was to take them past cheering crowds to Victoria station. Princess Elizabeth wore a powder-blue crepe, going-away dress and coat, also by Hartnell, which was topped off with a feathered blue beret by Thaarup. She was pregnant within three months of the marriage.

It is easy to forget, with all the fashion furore surrounding today's younger Royals, that this young couple provoked just as much excitement. Prince Philip told Gyles Brandreth that in the 1950s he and the Queen were subject to: "such adulation – you wouldn't believe it, you really wouldn't", and he went on to describe the Queen as "the world's sweetheart" with huge crowds fighting to catch a glimpse of her.

PAGE 31: Princess Elizabeth arrives at Westminster Abbey on the 20 November 1947, with her father, George VI, for her wedding to Lt. Philip Mountbatten (who was given the title Duke of Edinburgh). Norman Hartnell observed of his commission to design Princess Elizabeth's wedding dress: "I hoped this would be the most beautiful dress I had ever made." The Princess wore the historic Hanoverian diamond fringe tiara, inherited from George III.

H.A4.

HARDY AMIES LTD
16 Savile Row W.1.

NOVEMBER
1955
Albert Hall
Remembrance
Service

ABOVE AND OPPOSITE: Two stunning designs for the Queen from Hardy Amies.
Queen Elizabeth wore one to make her first live Christmas broadcast on television on
25 December 1957.

ABOVE: Queen Elizabeth meets Marilyn Monroe at the 1956 Royal Film Performance of *The Battle for River Plate*, in a dramatic, black velvet dress by Hartnell that showcases her fabulous jewellery. It is unusual for the Queen to wear black, but Hartnell wanted Her Majesty to outshine the film stars and not compete with them for glittering effect. OPPOSITE: Princess Elizabeth photographed at Clarence House, her marital home, in 1951, in a tulle and lace crinoline with silver thread by Norman Hartnell. In the same year President Truman commented: "When I was a little boy, I read about a fairy princess, and there she is." Her sapphire necklace and earrings, part of the King George VI Victorian Suite, were a wedding gift from her proud father.

# HATS

The Queen is very rarely seen without a hat, indeed it is such a significant feature that bookies take bets on what colour hat she will wear for each day of Ascot, as well as at Royal weddings. For this reason nobody knows what hat she will select for these occasions until she appears on the day.

Initially hats were an issue between couturier and dresser, for they were commissioned separately; Bobo (see page 8) wanted to retain control and used to remind couturiers that they were *only* responsible for the clothes, while she controlled the total ensemble. It took gentle pressure from the couturiers over the years for hats to be considered as part of the complete outfit and designed and made alongside the couture clothes.

Aage Thaarup, who was a favourite milliner of the Queen Mother, made many hats for the Queen in the 1940s and 1950s until he went bankrupt. Other Royal milliners include Simone Mirman for Hartnell, Freddie Fox for Amies, Valerie for Ian Thomas and Philip Summerville has worked with many couturiers more recently.

Freddie Fox was asked to make a hat for Queen Elizabeth for the first time in late 1969 for a trip to Argentina and Chile. "I made the hats myself, six designs", Freddie explains, "without telling anyone else what the commission was. Miss MacDonald (Bobo) and Miss Betty, from Amies, had a conference and finally gave me the head measurement. I'd only seen the Queen once and I worked with a postage stamp stuck to the workbench so that I could visualize her facial proportions."

The Queen's hats must function perfectly. She is known to take her milliners down to the Royal car to show them the problems she experiences getting in and out without her headwear being pushed askew. She will also sit in the car to show them where her head rests, for she must remain looking immaculate at all times. The Queen is reputed to boast that she has not lost a hat to the wind yet, although as photographs bear testament she has had to hold on to them on many occasions.

OPPOSITE: The Queen wears a hat of artificial leaves and berries and Queen Victoria's diamond stud earrings at a garden party at Freetown, Sierra Leone in November 1961.

ABOVE LEFT: The Queen wears a yellow, feathered hat and yellow, square-necked dress in St Kitts, 1966. ABOVE RIGHT: The Queen photographed by Eve Arnold in a svelte pink feathered, ribbon-trimmed toque in 1966. OPPOSITE: The Queen at the Epsom Derby in a stunning, white flowered toque in 1962.

# MOTHER

"THE QUEEN AND THE QUEEN MOTHER DO NOT WANT TO BE FASHION SETTERS, THAT'S LEFT TO OTHER PEOPLE WITH LESS IMPORTANT WORK TO DO. THEIR CLOTHES HAVE TO HAVE A NON SENSATIONAL ELEGANCE." NORMAN HARTNELL

# ✦ MOTHER ✦

The demands of being wife, mother and Princess are considerable; nevertheless the first four years of her marriage allowed Elizabeth more personal freedom than ever before, as she was not yet burdened with affairs of state. Elizabeth and Philip were relatively carefree, but it should be remembered that they were still Royal. Prince Charles had two Scottish nurses, even though Princess Elizabeth had declared: "I'm going to be the child's mother, not the nurses". Nevertheless, she had to attend to Royal duties, and while she was in London during the week, Charles remained with his nurses, firstly at Windlesham Moor in Berkshire and later at Clarence house when it had been redecorated. His parents returned home to see him at weekends. Cecil Beaton took the official portraits of the new baby: "The Princess, with wild-rose complexion, periwinkle-blue eyes, and a cool refreshing smile came in, followed by her nurse holding the precious bundle."

Motherhood brought a distinct change in Princess Elizabeth's wardrobe, for the first time she stopped dressing like a mirror-image of her mother, choosing much more distinctive tailored, full-skirted suits, which highlighted her tiny waist. She dressed like some other mothers of the period in neat suits, complemented with one or two pieces of good jewellery, although perhaps her suits were rather better tailored, and her good jewellery infinitely better than most. Major Charteris, Her Majesty the Queen's Private Secretary from 1950–77, told Gyles Brandreth how she looked when he met her for the first time: "She was wearing a blue dress and a brooch with huge sapphires. I was immediately struck by her bright blue eyes and her wonderful complexion. She was young, beautiful and dutiful. I knew at once that I would be proud to serve her."

Phillip and Elizabeth were regarded as a magical couple; Chips Cannon described seeing them at a ball at Windsor Castle at the end of Ascot in in 1949: "The Edinburghs made a somewhat late appearance (he had been to the Channel Islands or somewhere) and they looked divine. She wore a very high tiara and the Garter – he was in the dark blue

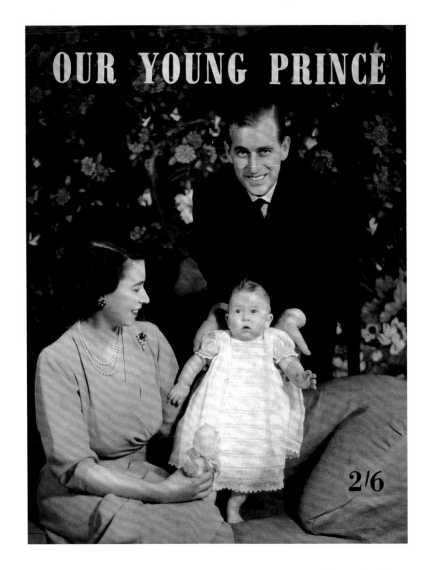

PREVIOUS PAGE: Cecil Beaton's picture of Princess Elizabeth with five-week-old Prince Charles taken in December 1948. She is wearing the flower basket brooch that her parents the King and Queen gave to her to celebrate the birth of their first grandchild. ABOVE: A souvenir magazine, *Our Young Prince*, is published in April 1949 to commemorate the birth of Prince Charles on 14 November 1948. It is the first published photograph of the family altogether.

Windsor uniform, also with the Garter. They looked like characters out of a fairy tale."

Despite being a young mother, Princess Elizabeth moved to Malta in Christmas 1949. She remained there with the Duke of Edinburgh – where he was made Lt. Commander of the frigate HMS *Magpie* – until the summer of 1951, although repeated trips home were required. In common with many service wives, the baby was left at home. Nevertheless, she and the Duke still had a considerable retinue; Bobo her dresser, an Equerry, a lady-in-waiting, a valet for the Duke and a detective. They stayed with family; the Mountbattens, who had a butler, housekeeper, three cooks, two housemaids, six stewards and two cleaning ladies to support themselves and the young couple.

It is perhaps at this time that the Duke of Edinburgh's young wife was at her most fashionable. In 1953 Norman Hartnell designed an elegant, slim-fitting, satin dress in black, with a white panel at the front (see page 67). Dubbed the "Magpie" dress by the press, it featured in most of the national papers and copies were quickly made and on sale by the next day. It was available in black and white, but also in a variety of colours, and within just a few days an impressive 120 copies had been sold. It was even turned into a paper pattern that cost the equivalent of 30p. Her Majesty never wore it again. She was also partial to Horrockses printed cotton dresses and whenever she was photographed in one the company would be swamped with orders.

The couturier Hardy Amies was approached by Princess Elizabeth in 1950 and described in his book, *Still Here*, how he planned to dress her in an updated New Look with shorter skirts: "just below the knee or certainly just above the calf … I already had the idea that royalty should be dressed like royalty, so I used rich materials. I also wanted to get away from the cliché of the pale-blue dress; at the same time blue was obviously going to be the Princesses's [sic] great colour, dictated by those oversized blue eyes."

Over the same period Princess Elizabeth also received the first criticism of her clothes. While sporting a temporarily fuller figure, as many young mothers do after the birth of their children, the American press accused her of being frumpish and the French press maintained that Englishwomen can look pretty, but never chic.

ABOVE LEFT: Princess Elizabeth in pale-blue organza with Princess Anne in 1951. ABOVE RIGHT: Princess Elizabeth and Princess Anne in an official christening portrait, October 1950. Elizabeth is in a tailored print dress, her diamond and sapphire brooch was her first official gift at the launch of the ship *British Princess* in 1946. Anne wears the Honiton lace robe, worn by members of the Royal family since 1841.

OPPOSITE: Queen Elizabeth in a beautiful tailored suit, with her children Charles and Anne at Balmoral in September 1952. The children are dressed identically, as she and her sister were. ABOVE: Queen Elizabeth in a glamorous, full-skirted, typically 1950s, silk frock, wearing the two-string pearl necklace that was originally part of the Hanoverian collection, and the Williamson pink diamond, which was made into a flower brooch in 1953, pictured here in December 1954. Charles and Anne are now dressed individually – Anne is in traditional girlish pink party frills and wears her mother's original pearl necklace.

ABOVE LEFT: The Royal family on a visit to Kincleven Church, Meiklous, Perthshire in October 1955. The Queen is wearing a slim-skirted, tailored suit and heels, despite the rough terrain. ABOVE RIGHT: The Queen favoured full-skirted, summer dresses for casual wear, as seen here at a polo match in Windsor with her family in June 1956. She frequently wore off-the-peg Horrockses designs, which sold out the moment she was seen in them, though hers were actually made-to-measure for her. OPPOSITE: Queen Elizabeth, in a tailored, full-skirted, floral suit, with Princess Anne in candy stripes at Windsor in May 1959.

THE Tatler

& Bystander    2s.6d.  weekly  26 Sept. 1962

OPPOSITE: Queen Elizabeth photographed at Windsor Castle for the September issue of *Tatler*, 1962. Note the ever present handbag at her side. Her Majesty is reputed to own some 200 handbags, which she uses again and again. Launer has had the royal warrant to supply her handbags for over forty years. ABOVE: A silver wedding anniversary photograph by Lord Lichfield in 1972 shows the Royal family on holiday in Balmoral, relaxed in tartan.

# TARTAN

The Royal family have always made a point of wearing Scottish tartans and tweeds to emphasize their heritage and home connections. The Balmoral Tartan, designed for Queen Victoria, should only be worn by the Royal family. ABOVE LEFT: Princesses Elizabeth and Margaret in the garden of the Royal Lodge, Windsor, in 1936, in typical play clothes of the time; short wool sweaters teamed with a kilt, white socks and sensible lace-up shoes. ABOVE RIGHT: Thirty-five years later, Queen Elizabeth is in much the same clothes and still in the company of corgis, here at Garbh Allt burn on the Balmoral estate, September 1971. OPPOSITE: The Royal family feature on the cover of *Woman's Own* magazine, April 1953, giving some heavy support to the Scottish textile industry.

# Woman's Own

4½D

The Royal Family
on holiday at Balmoral

*Wonderful* **EASTER HOLIDAY** *Reading* !

# DAY TO DAY

"I AM ONLY ONE OF THREE DESIGNERS WHO SUPPLY CLOTHES TO THE QUEEN.
EVEN MY THIRD OF THE WARDROBE TAKES SO MUCH TIME TO FIT THAT THERE IS
OFTEN GREAT DIFFICULTY IN FINDING TIME TO SQUEEZE THE FITTINGS INTO THE
QUEEN'S BUSY DIARY." HARDY AMIES

PREVIOUS PAGE: Queen Elizabeth in an exquisitely tailored, full-skirted, wool coat, is pictured with the Lady Mayoress on a visit to Berwick-on-Tweed in June 1958. ABOVE: Since her accession to the throne in 1952, Queen Elizabeth has had to deal with her red boxes of state papers, she is designated "Reader No. 1" and briefed on international matters as well as domestic politics. Even at work in the palace in 1958, she is a picture of timeless elegance in a dress that could be by contemporary designer Roland Mouret.

# DAY TO DAY

The Queen requires more clothes in a year than most of us do in a lifetime. Four or five changes per day are not unusual and her schedule is daunting. She makes openings, attends church services and garden parties, presents honours, visits hospitals, entertains visiting dignitaries, hosts banquets, as well as all her other daily, weekly and annual duties.

When new clothes are required the Queen's dresser simply telephones the couturier of choice and puts in a request for designs. Further information as to precisely what functions the clothes are needed for may not be forthcoming. This practice of either supplying, or withholding, relevant detail seems dependent upon the dresser in charge. Bobo used to brief designers, but in other instances designers were left to work in the dark. "We would receive a call from the dresser to say that the Queen would like to see some sketches – and that would be it, no more information", observes one couturier.[1] "We would speak to our PR and he would contact the palace press office, they in turn would speak to the Ladies-in-Waiting and try to glean what was going on. Was a tour planned and if so where and what time of year? For a designer it was so frustrating, you felt you could never do your best – it would have been so much better to have been given a brief, but we were never given one."

If the house had established that a tour was scheduled it could set about designing appropriately, although more generic designs would also be included. Creating couture design is an elaborate and time-consuming process, requiring careful planning and numerous fittings. It produces a custom-made garment, painstakingly constructed to conceal any physical flaws. Couture houses that work with Her Majesty over a long period of time will have a *vendeuse* who acts as overseer to the whole process. The in-house design team swings into action to create designs, these are pored over and fine-tuned in conversations with the Queen's *vendeuse* and the couturier, fabrics are selected or specially called in. "Everyone would put in their two pennorth…"[3] notes a designer who worked for Hardy Amies. "In those days we would call in an illustrator to produce polished drawings from our rough sketches, these would all have back views, typed descriptions and fabric swatches attached so that everything looked perfect, it was a huge amount of work. Then the *vendeuse* would call to ask for an appointment to meet the Queen."

The next stage in the process is for the couturier and the *vendeuse* to attend the palace with designs for Her Majesty to make a selection. "The Queen goes through the sketches very deliberately and she may sometimes ask for more information", a couturier explains.[1] "She then repeats the process indicating which designs she has selected. She is very quick and decisive." If the couturier is regularly commissioned by Her Majesty then garments in various stages of construction will also be fitted at the same appointment. Fitting each ensemble can take between 15 and 30 minutes.

Once the designs have been selected work can begin. Couture houses keep a mannequin for the Queen's clothes. At Amies this was known as "The Queen's Dummy" and adjusted to reflect her changing shape over the years. It is her to her credit that one couturier notes: "She remains pretty stable and is wonderfully upright, but occasionally we would have a bit of a panic in the taxi after a fitting because her shape had altered."[3]

At Hardy Amies the Queen had her own dressmaker, Miss Lillian, and tailor, Mr Michael, who cut the toiles – fabric mock-ups, often constructed in cotton calico, for the first fitting and sometimes lined for comfort. This is a prudent practice because if fabric is expensive, which in couture it generally is, no risks can be taken with the actual cloth. By the second fitting the garment is constructed in its correct fabric and fine-tuned for perfect fit. The *vendeuse* contacts a selected milliner, indicating the design and fabric chosen, so that they can also attend the second fitting with a selection of hats for consideration. At the third and final fitting the dress should not require any adjustments, save the hem, and Her Majesty tries on the completed design with her choice of shoes, bag and hat to ensure that everything works.

One *vendeuse* notes: "Fittings were always very easy. She was marvellous to deal with and amazingly patient. Everything was always laid on beautifully for us – it was a joy and an honour to look after her."[2] Standing, being fitted, fussed over and pinned is a very wearing process. Several couturiers confirm that the Queen tests her clothes out carefully at fittings; she waves, sits and considers how easy it will be to move in them when going up and down stairs. And while Her Majesty the Queen is always observed to be appreciative, there is generally no feedback from her.

ABOVE: Norman Hartnell designed this coat of white grosgrain, edged with navy blue. It was first worn by Her Majesty at the Coronation Review of the Fleet at Spithead, and then later, here, in Wales in 1953. OVERLEAF: The Queen is a perfect 1950s fashion plate in a tiny hat and voluminous duster coat on a visit to a war veteran in Scotland in July 1953.

Fittings are a daunting process and most couturiers and milliners confirm that the first visit is terrifying. Frederick Fox explains that he was carefully briefed by Hardy Amies in advance: "*Don't* touch the Queen, *don't* ask questions and *don't* turn your back", he was instructed. Come the day, "the Queen was standing at the end of a long room, I advanced, did my chat and my thing. When it was time to depart I was rooted to the spot, I thought that if I walked backwards I would fall over the furniture or one of the corgis. Her Majesty spotted my dilemma and turned her back on me to ask Bobo to fetch some specific shoes – giving me the opportunity to withdraw."

Bobo, described in her obituary in *The Guardian* in September 1993 as "the scourge of milliners and couturiers", curtailed the influence of designers, ensuring that no single couture house could exert a monopoly. She made it clear that while they designed the dresses, regarding accessories – shoes, handbags and hats – were commissioned elsewhere. Hardy Amies, complained bitterly about ugly handbags, stating plainly that they were ruining his beautiful designs. He, along with other couturiers, adopted the practice of giving Her Majesty tastefully chosen handbags as Christmas presents in the hope they might be utilized.

Most couturiers maintain a record of everything they make for Her Majesty. At Hardy Amies this item was commonly known as The Queen's Book: "this was my bible", one *vendeuse* explains. "It contained a record of everything that was made and when. It detailed the fabric, where it came from, and for reference purposes fabric swatches were pinned in. This was necessary because we might make a coat and dress for her, the dress might be in silk, and three years later she might ask for another dress to be made to go with the coat and I had all the relevant information. The book was very precious."

But the privilege of servicing the Queen comes at a cost: as one couturier observes: "Just in man hours it is terribly expensive – four members of staff out of the office all afternoon, sometimes on a weekly basis, let alone the man hours in making the clothes, as well as the extra care and effort that went into every single thing we did. There was an enormous pride in the house that we were making things for the Queen, it was a huge privilege, but with that privilege came a lot of responsibility and those expenses had to get absorbed."[1] It is perhaps worth noting that it is not unknown for the Queen's suppliers to go out of business.

ABOVE: Princess Elizabeth receives the Freedom of the City of London in her first significant unaccompanied ceremony on 11 June 1947. RIGHT: The Queen isnpects the Grenadier Guards in July 1968.

ABOVE: Queen Elizabeth talks to Dr Adenauer, the West German Chancellor, at Windsor Castle in April 1958. Her exquisite embroidered evening gown shows off her tiny waist. Richard Crossman describes her as: "this little woman with the beautiful waist".

OPPOSITE: The Hartnell "Magpie" dress in black and white satin, that Her Majesty wore to a Royal Command Film Performance of the musical *Because You're Mine* at Leicester Square. The dress was copied and in the shops within twenty-four hours. (See page 46.)

ABOVE LEFT: Queen Elizabeth in a lemon lace two-piece, with corsage, wide-brimmed hat and sunglasses, arrives at Windsor Great Park for a cocktail party given by the 1st Battalion of the Irish Guards. ABOVE RIGHT: Queen Elizabeth reflects the changing shape of fashion in a slimmer-fitting, floral-print dress with bow detail, teamed with white accessories, pictured with her mother at Ascot in June 1960. OPPOSITE: The Queen takes a good look at the parade of the Oaks runners dressed in an immaculate dress and coat suit with feathered hat, in June 1962.

ABOVE: The Queen, photographed in 1976, displays typical 1970s fashion detailing, including a large teardrop collar and waist belt. The same coat was worn to Lord Lichfield's wedding a year earlier. She also wears Empress Marie Feodorovna of Russia's cabochon sapphire, diamond and pearl brooch. OPPOSITE: Queen Elizabeth in a slim, blue, tailored suit, with matching feathered hat and black accessories, arrives at a wet Aberdeen airport, complete with corgis, to start her holidays at Balmoral in 1972.

ABOVE: Queen Elizabeth is often described as a countrywomen at heart, certainly her off-duty wardrobe combines all the finest aspects of country style: tailored tweeds, quilted jackets, simple knitwear and the perennial favourite, the silk square. Here the Queen watches Prince Philip driving Four-In-Hand at the Windsor Horse Show in 1984. OPPOSITE: The Queen at Balmoral in her beautifully tailored riding clothes.

ABOVE: Queen Elizabeth leaves a Service of Celebration to mark 400 years of the King James Bible, held at Westminster Abbey in November 2011. Her Majesty wears a cream, raised woven fabric coat designed by her Senior Dresser, Angela Kelly. The matching hat is by Rachel Trevor-Morgan. OPPOSITE: Queen Elizabeth wears a couture design by Sandra Murray for the opening of the Scottish Parliament in July 1999. The silk and wool frockcoat is worn over a wool-crepe dress overlaid with lace. The Isle of Skye tartan plaid is secured by Her Majesty's Oban brooch. The hat is by Philip Somerville; the gloves, shoes and bag were specially made to match – the breakaway ensemble was hailed as a style triumph.

# SHOES

The family firm of Rayne first acquired a Royal Warrant in 1936, courtesy of Queen Mary, an honour that was to be repeated by Queen Elizabeth The Queen Mother and Queen Elizabeth. Rayne shoes are delicate, beautifully designed and, this is key, exquisitely comfortable; a major consideration for royalty who spend long hours on their feet.

After the Second World War, when Edward Rayne joined the company, it became the most glamorous shoe brand in Europe, supplying the likes of Marlene Dietrich, Elizabeth Taylor, Vivien Leigh and Diana Rigg, as well as the Royal family Rayne worked with designers such as Roger Vivier, Jean Muir, Mary Quant, Bill Gibb and Bruce Oldfield, in addition to both British and French couturiers.

Edward Rayne caused royal consternation early in his career on a trip to New York in 1947 when he accidentally revealed Her Majesty's shoe size to a journalist at a cocktail party; a detail deemed so fascinating that it was splashed across newspapers in the United States and Britain. Mr Rayne was summoned to the palace and asked how he could have been so indiscreet. Nevertheless, he must have been forgiven for he continued to make shoes for the Queen for forty years. He made her wedding shoes – three pairs were produced in case of disaster – and her Coronation shoes, which were designed by Roger Vivier at Her Majesty's special request.

Edward Rayne attended the Queen four to six times a year, generally when shoes were required for tours, or state occasions, and these were carefully created to complement the couturier's designs, as the selection of sketches for a tour of Holland in 1958 (opposite) indicates. Nevertheless, Her Majesty is no Imelda Marcos; shoes were carefully looked after and worn as long as practical, although there were occasional problems, as any dog owner will know to their cost. Her Majesty's corgis are no exception and the Queen would occasionally produce a pair with a chewed heel and ask Mr Rayne if he might be able repair the problem.

H.M. THE QUEEN
FOR STATE TOUR. HOLLAND 1958

Her Majesty the Queen. Black calf pump by Rayne
with calf button securing tab treatment on vamp.

H.M. THE QUEEN.
FOR STATE TOUR. HOLLAND 1958

Her Majesty the Queen. Blue crepe halter-back
sandal by Rayne with ¾" platform. The whole of
the sandal is decorated with Mother-of-Pearl sequins.

H.M. THE QUEEN
FOR STATE TOUR. HOLLAND 1958

Her Majesty the Queen. Off-white satin closed-back
open-toe shoe by Rayne with ¾" platform; rhinestone
treatment on vamp.

H.M. THE QUEEN.
FOR STATE TOUR. HOLLAND 1958

Her Majesty the Queen. Mid-brown calf pump by
Rayne with trimming in same material.

ABOVE: Rayne was one of the most celebrated British shoe designers. The company
produced shoes for Wallis Simpson, Queen Elizabeth The Queen Mother, Princess
Margaret, Princess Anne and Princess Diana as well as Her Majesty. The sketches pictured
here were made for Queen Elizabeth's Tour of Holland in 1958.

# STATE
# OCCASIONS

"SHE DID NOT FIND IT DEMEANING TO BE A DOLL DRESSED FOR HER SUBJECTS'
PLEASURE. SHE SAW IT AS THE ESSENCE OF HER JOB. THE HOLY PUPPET CLOTHED
IN MAGIC ROBES FOR THE PEOPLES' COMFORT WENT BACK TO THE VERY ROOTS OF
PRIMEVAL MONARCHY." ROBERT LACEY

# STATE OCCASIONS

The Queen began her reign on 6 February 1952 in an outfit none of us associate with her. She was in Sagana Lodge in Kenya when she was given the news that her father had died. She had been up since dawn watching the wildlife and was wearing jeans. Still in jeans when she left the Lodge for Nanyuki to start the long journey home, she flew from here to Entebbe where the Royal party were reunited with the rest of the luggage, which had been flown up from Mombasa – including the black mourning clothes that had been packed by Bobo to guard against this very eventuality. She emerged from the aircraft, a small figure in black, and was met on the tarmac at Heathrow by Prime Minister Winston Churchill.

In October 1952 Her Majesty asked Norman Hartnell to design her Coronation gown. She requested a dress in white satin that conformed in line to that of her wedding gown. After exhaustive research, Hartnell offered eight designs ranging from severe to elaborate. The eighth sketch utilized national emblems: the Tudor Rose, the shamrock, the thistle and the daffodil, although Hartnell learned, to his despair, that the leek, not the daffodil, was the national emblem of Wales. His design was amended accordingly and the Queen requested that the emblems of all her dominions should also be included: the maple leaf, the fern, acacia, protea, lotus, wheat, cotton and jute. The final ninth design and sample embroideries were deemed to be perfect, save that the green used for the shamrock should be more subdued.

The emblems were embroidered in pale silk and highlighted with pearls, crystals and opals to create an iridescent sheen. Unknown to the Queen, Hartnell added one small detail of his own, on the left-hand side of the skirt he had one four-leafed shamrock embroidered for luck. The garment was technically difficult to make and the stiff, bejewelled and weighty skirt would not move correctly, so it was lined with cream taffeta, and reinforced with three layers of horsehair crinoline, to give a dignified gentle movement. At the final fitting Her Majesty's verdict was: "Glorious", but she warned Cecil Beaton, who was to take the official photographs, that: "There are layers upon layers: skirt and mantle and

Norman Hartnell.

PAGE 78: Her Majesty arrives at Westminster Abbey for her Coronation on 2 June 1953. PREVIOUS PAGE: The shimmering opulence of the Coronation gown stunned onlookers. The glittering Imperial State Crown is set with 2,873 diamonds, 273 pearls, 17 sapphires, 11 emeralds and five rubies. ABOVE: Unbeknown to Her Majesty, Norman Hartnell had a single four-leaf shamrock embroidered where her left hand would brush against it. Her shoes were designed by the French footwear designer Roger Vivier.

trains." The dress weighed an impressive 30 lb (13.6 kg). Hartnell also designed a "simple" white lawn gown, with a deep collar, a bodice hand-tucked on the cross, and a sunray pleated skirt. This garment, required for the Anointing ceremony, slipped over Her Majesty's Coronation gown and fastened simply at the back.

The Queen rehearsed in the State Ballroom with sheets attached to her shoulders, to simulate the weight of her robes. She also rehearsed wearing the heavy, 5 lb (2.2 kg) St Edward's Crown, as she had seen her father do before her. Hartnell's gown was deemed to be a masterpiece. In his book, *The Strenuous Years,* Cecil Beaton describes the impact the Queen had at her Coronation: "The cheeks are sugar-pink: her hair tightly curled around the Victorian diadem of precious stones straight on her brow. Her pink hands are folded meekly on the elaborate grandeur of her encrusted skirt; she is still a young girl with a demeanour of simplicity and humility. Perhaps her mother has taught her never to use a superfluous gesture. As she walks she allows her heavy skirt to sing backwards and forwards in a beautiful rhythmic effect. This girlish figure has enormous dignity; she belongs in this scene of almost Byzantine magnificence."

State occasions represent an opportunity for her Majesty to wear her most ornate evening gowns, and her best jewellery. At the end of a state occasion she used to remark to Bobo, her dresser, "I gave them my best bits", referring to her jewellery. In addition to the jewels there may well be insignia: Orders, Collars, Badges and Garter sashes, which have been known to cause a sartorial crisis – the most notable occasion being in Japan when an emerald green dress was teamed with a red sash, edged in blue. The Queen often wears Royal Family Orders pinned to her sash; a family tradition, started by George IV, of wearing miniatures of each other.

These most formal of occasions also see the Queen in full dress uniform; she is Colonel-in-chief of the Household regiments and has a critical eye for accuracy in military apparel. Official robes, such as the heavy Garter robes worn at the Celebration of the Solemnity of the Garter, are maintained and occasionally replaced. At the State Opening of Parliament Her Majesty wears the Parliament Robe of State and dons the Imperial State Crown. She is reputed to be happier in uniform than any other style of dress. An ex-courtier told Ben Pimlott: "She used to be fanatical about getting into training for Trooping the Colour. Two month's beforehand she would start losing weight because she had to fit into the uniform."

ABOVE: The Queen attends the Trooping of the Colour ceremony in June 1951, riding side saddle. Her uniform and riding skirt are made by Bernard Weatherill. OPPOSITE: The Queen wears the insignia and mantle of the Order of the Garter, – the oldest Order of Chivalry in Britain, – in the annual Garter service in June at St George's Chapel, Windsor. Her robes are made by Ede & Ravenscroft on Savile Row.

OPPOSITE: The Queen wears a magnificent white and silver beaded dress in her Coronation Year, 1953. She is wearing The Order of the Garter, the oldest Order of Chivalry in the world, as well as the Royal Family Orders; miniatures of her father and grandfather set in diamonds on pieces of moiré silk. ABOVE: Queen Elizabeth loved Karsh Yousef's photographs of her, describing them as "delicious". Here she is wearing an embroidered duchesse satin dress, with asymmetric neckline, by Norman Hartnell.

H.A.10.

*Canada Tour '59*

ABOVE AND OPPOSITE: Norman Hartnell and Hardy Amies together created such a strong image for the Queen that it was sometimes hard to tell whose designs were whose. Compare the stunning illustration (above) of a Hardy Amies design for the Royal tour of Canada in 1959, with Hartnell's slim-fitting dress (opposite) with tulle, fan-tailed bustle worn in New York in October 1957 – it sparkled magnificently under the Kleig runway lights as she departed by plane.

ABOVE: Queen Elizabeth in a Hartnell dress for Princess Margaret's wedding on 6 May 1960. It was the last time that the Queen wore a full-length dress to a wedding. She wears the "Lover's Knot" diamond brooch that was left to her by her grandmother Queen Mary. OPPOSITE: Lord Lichfield took this photograph of Queen Elizabeth leaving Buckingham Palace in the Irish State Coach on her way to State Opening of Parliament in 1971. She is wearing a Hartnell, mink-trimmed, silver and white coat created for her state visit to France in 1972. Four different dresses were made to go underneath it.

# ✦ FURS ✦

ABOVE: The Queen arrives at a Royal Variety Performance in 1960 in a curved and shaped fur stole, which she has worn repeatedly throughout her reign. Princess Elizabeth was brought up wearing furs in the days when it was socially acceptable to do so. Today she is highly selective and only wears a few favourite pieces to special occasions. OPPOSITE: On a tour of India in 1961 she gave a speech to an estimated crowd of 250,000 in Old Delhi.

# ON TOUR

"SHE DOESN'T DO FASHION — SHE IS THE LAST ONE INTO A FASHION AND THE LAST ONE OUT OF IT, BUT HER APPEARANCE IS VERY IMPORTANT TO HER AND SHE IS VERY DEVOTED TO HER JOB." FREDERICK FOX

# ON TOUR

The work and planning that goes into any Royal tour is phenomenal, each requires months of preparation and every detail of the trip is organized and timed. Clothes are specially commissioned and while these may be worn to a vast array of functions for years afterwards, it would be considered undiplomatic if they were not brand new for the tour. The Queen and her clothes must be seen to complement her hosts, as well as being respectful of the culture and local conventions. In advance of a trip to Saudi Arabia in February 1970, the Queen wrote to Hardy Amies: "I'm told 'no bare flesh' is the main concern" Amies dutifully concealed her arms and legs.

Once everything has been finalized the details are printed in a small, pocket-sized booklet called *The Blue Book* – known unofficially as "The Bible". This is carried by every member of the household concerned with the visit. Every last detail is listed, including the clothes to be worn at each event. A capital letter "T" besides the Queen's name indicates that she will be wearing a tiara. Her Majesty has learned to be a master of quick changes, as many as six outfits per day can be required, she is often seen putting on her tiara in the corridor on route to her next function.

A mountain of luggage is assembled and, unlike that of film stars, it is neither elegant nor immaculate, but rather a motley assortment of trunks, cases, zip bags and hatboxes. Their only single defining feature is that each bears the words "The Queen" on the side. The weight must be immense, but Her Majesty's luggage is never weighed. Clothes are beautifully packed and sent ahead so that they are all ready and waiting on arrival. Tours are exhausting for dressers, who are permanently packing, unpacking and ironing. The Queen's jewellery travels with her in a special leather case, and is the responsibility of her personal footman, who returns it to the care of the dresser at its destination. On the New Zealand leg of Her Majesty's first tour of the Commonwealth (1953–4) it was discovered that her jewels were missing. There was always the possibility that the bag had accidentally been put with the rest of the luggage, which was already airborne. One can only imagine the relief when, on arrival at Government

PREVIOUS PAGE: Queen Elizabeth, in a chic yellow dress and flowerpot hat, is protected from the sun under a giant umbrella in Ghana, November 1960. ABOVE LEFT: On other women a skirt catching the breeze would count as a wardrobe malfunction, but the Queen ensures that such problems never occur. Her couturier Maureen Rose explains the secret: "I always put in a straight lining, fitted to the body, so that even if the dress blew up, the lining wouldn't." Here she is returning from a visit to Canada in August 1959. ABOVE RIGHT: The Queen always dresses appropriately; trousers are required for a tiger shoot with King Mahendra of Nepal in March 1961, although Her Majesty did not participate.

House in Wellington, the jewel case was discovered, together with the rest of the household luggage.

Her Majesty's first foreign tour was a trip to South Africa and Rhodesia in 1947, until then she had not set foot outside the United Kingdom. Clothes rationing was still causing problems so Hartnell utilized some of the her mother's pre-war clothes as material for her dresses. A rare wardrobe malfunction occurred on a trip to Cecil Rhodes' grave in the Matopos Hills, Bulawayo; the Queen realized that her high-heeled, peep-toed shoes were completely unsuitable and she could not continue. Princess Elizabeth saved the day by giving her mother her own more sensible shoes, and undertaking the rest of the climb in stockinged feet.

A little over a year later she made an unofficial visit to Paris. Her mother had scored a fashion triumph eleven years earlier wearing an all-white wardrobe, designed by Hartnell; Princess Elizabeth and her new husband had a similar impact. At a gala evening she sparkled in a diamond tiara and necklace, a wedding gift from the Nizam of Hyderbad, and was said by her Private Secretary Jock Colville to have "conquered Paris".

Just four months after the Coronation, in November 1953, the Queen and the Duke of Edinburgh embarked on a huge five and a half month tour of the Commonwealth. Charles and Anne were left behind. The trip included banquets, troop inspections, parliament openings and state occasions and required a huge wardrobe – 150 dresses no less – which Norman Hartnell and Hardy Amies had been commissioned to work on months in advance. The day wear was chic and discreet, evening dresses glittered with beads and embroidery. For the human touch there were even some Horrockses ready-to-wear dresses among the couture grandeur.

The weather must always be a consideration when clothes are prepared for Royal tours. The Queen wrote to Amies regarding a planned trip to South east Asia in 1972: "I find every time I read a programme for the Far East Tour, I get hotter and hotter at the prospect of six weeks in that climate." It has been confirmed that *sousdebra*, a form of detachable underarm padding designed to absorb perspiration, are utilized in the Royal wardrobe when deemed appropriate. But, despite all this careful preparation, last-minute changes of outfit still occur; flimsy dresses are replaced if a sudden downpour looks likely, or a tailored coat-suit abandoned in a heat wave. It is perhaps reassuring to note that despite everything, Her Majesty, like the rest of us, is still affected by the weather.

PREVIOUS PAGE: Queen Elizabeth wears Norman Hartnell's heavy, black-and-white satin "Magpie" coat-dress for a State visit to Paris in April 1957. Dresses from Hartnell's collections were withdrawn from sale if selected by the Queen. ABOVE: Queen Elizabeth in a pleated chiffon dress at a garden party in Melbourne in March 1954. Both Hartnell and Amies designed for the Queen on this tour. OPPOSITE: Hardy Amies designed this glamorous, fitted, white lace dress for the Queen's tour of Australia and New Zealand in 1953–54. It has the understated elegance of the designs favoured by Grace Kelly.

OPPOSITE: The incredible glamour of the young Queen Elizabeth won approval from the Americans in New York City in 1957. ABOVE LEFT: Queen Elizabeth arrives at a state reception in Paris in April 1957, *Picture Post* reported: "The Queen Conquers France." ABOVE RIGHT: This gold-lamé and lace, one-shouldered evening was designed by Hartnell for the Queen's extended Commonwealth tour. She is pictured here in Wellington, New Zealand in 1954.

ABOVE: Queen Elizabeth in a stunning gold dress and hat at a costume parade in Karachi during the Royal Tour of India in January 1961. OPPOSITE: On the same trip the Queen wears a lavender dress and duster coat to a civic ceremony in New Delhi. All Her Majesty's gloves are supplied by Cornelia James; she can wear as many as five pairs a day. Her preference is for suede fabric gloves that can be easily cleaned and dyed.

OPPOSITE: Queen Elizabeth works florals in a stunning piece of 1960s design and tailoring on a trip to Malta in November 1967. ABOVE: Norman Hartnell designed loose coats with matching dresses, which became Queen Elizabeth's trademark look, to help her manage the heat on her tour of India in 1961

# JEWELS

ABOVE LEFT: Queen Elizabeth can carry off bling, which she describes with delicious understatement as her "best bits", like no one else. Here, in Ethiopia in 1965, the Queen is wearing Queen Victoria's Collet and Queen Alexandra's Russian Kokoshnik Tiara, encrusted with 488 diamonds. ABOVE RIGHT: The Queen wears the Cambridge Lover's Knot Tiara and Queen Victoria's Jubilee diamond and pearl necklace. OPPOSITE: The Queen in the King George IV State Diadem en route to the Opening of Parliament, 1952.

# BIBLIOGRAPHY

**Amies** Hardy, *Still Here*, Weidenfeld & Nicholson, 1984

**Beaton** Cecil, *The Glass of Fashion*, Weidenfeld & Nicholdson, 1954

**Beaton** Cecil, *Photobiography*, Odhams Press Limited, 1951

**Beaton** Cecil, *The Years Between*, Weidenfeld & Nicholson, 1965

**Beaton** Cecil, *Beaton in the Sixties*, Weidenfeld & Nicholson, 2003

**Beaton Cecil**, *The Unexpurgated Beaton*, Weidenfeld & Nicholson, 2002

**Bradford** Sarah, *Elizabeth*, Penguin books, 2002

**Brandreth** Gyles, *Philip and Elizabeth*, Century, 2004

**Crawford** Marion, *The Little Princesses*, Cassell & Co Ltd, 1950

**Dampier** Phil and **Walton** Ashley, *What's in the Queen's Handbag*, Book Guild Ltd, 2007

**Edwards** Anne, *The Queen's Clothes*, Beaverbrook Newspapers Limited, 1976

**Field** Leslie, *The Queen's Jewels*, Times Mirror Books, Harry N. Abrams, 1987

**Hartnell** Norman, *Silver and Gold*, Evans Brothers Limited, 1955

**Hoey** Brian, *Life with the Queen*, Sutton Publishing Ltd, 2006

**Lacey** Robert, *Royal: Her Majesty Queen Elizabeth II*, Little, Brown, 2002

**Laver** James, *The Place of Crowning*, John Mowlem and Company, 1953

**Longford** Elizabeth, *Elizabeth R*, Weidenfeld and Nicholson, 1983

**Marr** Andrew, *The Diamond Queen*, Macmillan, 2011

**McDowell** Colin, *A Hundred Years of Royal Style*, Muller, Blond & White, 1985

**Menkes** Susie, *The Royal Jewels*, Grafton Books, 1985

**Moorhouse** Paul, *The Queen Art & Image*, National Portrait Gallery, 2011

**Morrow** Ann, *The Queen*, Book Club Associates, 1983

**Patterson** Stephen, *Royal Insignia*, Merrell Holberton, 1996

**Pick** Michael, *Be Dazzled*, Pointed Leaf Press, 2007

**Pimlott** Ben, *The Queen*, Harper Collins Publishers, 2001

**Vickers** Hugo, *Cecil Beaton*, Weidenfeld & Nicholson, 1985

**Zeigler** Philip, *Queen Elizabeth II*, Thames & Hudson, 2010

*Five Gold Rings*, Royal Collections Enterprises Ltd, 2007

*Happy & Glorious*, Angus & Robertson, 1977

*Queen Elizabeth II*, Royal Collection Publications, 2006

# ACKNOWLEDGEMENTS

I have had a great deal of assistance in writing this book from a number of people who work in couture. Most asked to speak off the record, not I hasten to add because they were in any way critical of Her Majesty; even speaking off the record they were only ever full of praise. They spoke to me to help ensure that this book is factually correct and for their consideration and generosity I am profoundly grateful. I would also like to take this opportunity to thank the couturiers and milliners who spoke on the record, and the House of Hardy Amies who kindly enabled me to look at their archive and who were generous enough to allow their illustrations to be reproduced in this book. I must offer a special thank you to Frederick Fox, I am indebted to him for his kindness and his great wit. As always, thanks go to Sarah Gristwood for her support and advice. I would also like to thank my editor Emily Preece-Morrison and Polly Powell at Anova for their faith in me, Emma O'Neill for finding such fabulous pictures, and Georgie Hewitt for her superb design.

**Chapter notes**

Introduction

1: Confidential interview with couturier, see acknowledgements.

Chapter 4

1: Confidential interview with couturier A, see acknowledgements.

2: Confidential interview with *vendeuse*, see acknowledgements.

3: Confidential interview with couturier B, see acknowledgements.

Chapter 5

\* Most biographies of Queen Elizabeth II maintain that she received the news of the death of her father and her ascension to the throne while wearing jeans. Elizabeth Longford, who has impeccable credentials, maintains that Her Majesty was wearing a white dress.

# PICTURE CREDITS